JAMILLAH LONDON

FROM HURT 2 HEALING

Dedication

I dedicate this book to my daughter's, grandchildren, family and friends. Everyone who lost family members and friends to Covid 19

A good friend of mine, Lisa Burhanon.

Cousin in law Alfreda Bellamy

My Aunt Doris(Dot) Banks who passed on my Birthday 12/15/2020

Acknowledgements

I would like to thank Sharif Layton my co writer for his inspiration and Encouragement.

The Mission for H.E.A.L

Our mission at H.E.A.L. is to show people (who have been victimized) that they are worthy and deserve to be loved. We know that love is the center of creating a healthy life and at H.E.A.L. we are facilitating the achieving of love to enhance life, create unity and promote harmony

The Anthem

Let us break bread like Jesus did and share the love we should

reciprocate what we've received putting us at ease.

We need to help relieve the pressure that our folks are

feeling from a lack of love .

We have to help fill that empty space with love. As

we've been blessed we also need to bless others.

We are here to help one another.

We must spread love like light when the sun rises , we

must radiate warmth and help people see that there are no

I's there is only We.

Contents

Finding Purpose after hurt   1

Seeing the need to heal   5

Choosing to Heal to become a better you   8

Seeking Help   12

Analyzing the Hurt   16

Shame   20

Fear   23

Acceptance   27

Focus   31

Finding Purpose after hurt

I was devastated when I lost my son. No one could tell me how and when to stop grieving. I knew I would never forget the day I lost him to gun violence. Going through this kind of hurt is almost indescribable. It is literally the fight of your life and like fighting, it is enlightening. Creating a unique view that will tend to reshape the ways you look at life, that perspective will position you for your ultimate mission and assist in finding purpose. Finding purpose is personal and is usually based upon something that you are passionate about. People may recommend what they feel will fit you, but ultimately it is up to you to decide and find the purpose for you. You know yourself, find and embrace your calling and go global. Hurt cannot live there anymore. Let go of the pain that is draining you. Humanity has a tendency to hold on , to collect and in the extreme hoard.

Many unknowingly choose to hold onto hurtful things that have the tendency to drain ones vitality. You must learn to let go so that you can grab onto the beautiful things that are coming your way. In particular drop pain so that you can embrace healing. Letting go consists of realizing that you are continuing to carry a rock that is robbing you of your vitality. You are unable to see and participate in the life you want because you are preoccupied. You are holding on as if your life only consists of the event or the events that created the pain, that you are taking everywhere you go. Know that it is ok to let go. You do not have to carry the burden and out of all things, those burdens are those that have been weighing you down.

Your hurt and pain is not supposed to be permanent, know that subconsciously you chose to carry it when you can choose to release it.

Realize that you do not have to hurt. Become aware and be mindful of what you have become accustomed to. Realize that pain is a part of life, but persistent pain is not normal.

Living a hurt life is not normal. Feeling helpless consistently is not normal What is normal is, you becoming conscious and adjusting to make your life better. The new normal consists of you realizing that you refuse to hold onto hurt, as it has already been proven to be toxic to your well-being, both mentally and physically. You are and have always been in the driver's seat.

You have been tolerating hurt because you were not aware of the power you have. Awareness must become the impetus to liberating yourself and breaking free of the perception of helplessness, to becoming mindful that you are powerful. It is no longer possible to continue holding on. You now should know that you have the power to let go. Refuse to continue embracing that wretched state of existence. Release the hurt and move towards healing, it was never necessary to carry it.

Seeing the need to heal

Sometimes the experience of hurt is so profound that we are seemingly forced to mask it and to cope not knowing that the simmering hurt will eventually reach a flashpoint culminating in recurring explosions. As we continue to feed the beast, we become oblivious to the crisis that exist within. Our only solace seems to be when we are indulging to suppress the pain. We have learned and have become experts at covering our hurt, unaware of the mental and anatomical damage that we are inflicting on ourselves. Covering does not negate the presence of pain, just like a hidden ticking time bomb remains a bomb. We need awareness, we must become aware of the source of our hurt. We must look into and address our issues. It is amazing how we will service our car when the 'check engine' light turns on, yet when we are in a crisis, we do not seek service for our mental and emotional needs. It is time to act, we cannot allow hurt to restrict us, and hurt cannot be permitted to hold us hostage.

As healing is possible, we must look at our lives and in the true spirit of criticism, check ourselves. We must question our motivation; ask why do I continue to do this? we must be honest, we must confront our hurt if we are to heal. We will discover that healing is a possibility seeing the possibility is like opening a new world. We must go on and explore.

Choosing to Heal to become a better you

Choose to heal, choose to remove hurt, and choose to improve. It is natural to desire to be the best you. As the veil has been removed it's finally possible. The obstacle has always been mental as you have always held the helm. It was the lack of awareness that left you locked in. Fortunately, things have changed and you are feeling the power that you have. Go for your goals and get your gold. Heal and once you have, give someone else a helping hand. Going through this kind of hurt is almost Indescribable, giving you a unique view that will tend to reshape the way that you look at life .

Find the courage to begin the journey. Finding developing courage is like everything else. Its built on practice, keep attempting until you develop it . Simply speaking ,you must take chances. You must realize that fear is just your imagination . Imagining the worst and at the same time holding you back . Visualize and see yourself succeeding. Know that the road to healing begins with the first step that you've already concluded.

held you, so stop sitting in self-pity and start stepping on your journey to healing you.

Seeking Help

You are not an island, as you embark on your journey of healing, you will need help. If you are not accustomed to reaching out, know that it will behoove you to turn over a new leaf and start now. Seeking help begins with a new humbleness which consists of you realizing that you do not have all the answers and that there are people who have been where you would like to go. Your task is to find and connect with those people and learn from their experiences. Seeking help is a part of a massive paradigm shift that consists of changing the perspective you see the world through.

The shift will permit you to free yourself of those previously conceived notions that have left you conflicted and restricted on the deep sea of afflictions. You must begin to see that you have the power. You always have options. Things do not have to be the way they are. The myth is that you are powerless. The truth is that you are powerful! Seeking help will allow you to access the door leading to relieving of the pain that has been draining you. It has always been up to you. You have always had the potential, yet the view you saw life through was not conducive to your wellbeing. Reach out, seek help, build the bridges and cross over into the land where hurt cannot hold you anymore. It is senseless to continue hurting when you can begin healing.

Rethink how you have been seeing yourself, how do you view yourself? Have you even considered who you are? Going through the journey of hurt to healing has certainly shed new light and given you new insight. Are you surprised by what you see? Are you surprised by what and how you think now? Has there been a change? Or are you reluctant, afraid to go down that path, paralyzed by fear? Would it hurt to work on you ?

What could be better than becoming a better person? If you are not happy adjust . Be like water unable to be permanently restricted or confined . Water always finds its way through and so should you. continue to consider and critique what you see when you view yourself and make the necessary adjustments to bring out the best in you .

Analyzing the Hurt

Has it set in you that you need to heal? It set in me that I needed to heal when I felt like I was losing my mind. When did you decide to commit to healing? I decided to commit to healing when I realized I had two other children left to take care of. What is wrong with the way that you see yourself? I have seen myself as if I lost a battle as a mother. What has changed, regarding the way you see yourself? My goal was that I have always wanted to help people; how can I help people heal if I am not healed? What are you going to be doing differently that you have not been doing mentally? Change my way of thinking. Changing my way of thinking.

Interacting with Jamillah

Seeking help

What made you realize that you needed help?

I tried to suppress my emotions in an uncomfortable way.

Do you have a support system?

I had a support system after I lost my son. I expected to have more supporters.

Are you actively reaching out for help?

I reached out for help whenever needed and by doing this it made my healing process easier.

Are you willing to help others?

I am willing to help others because I know the process one has to go through in order to heal.

Hurt

How did you see yourself improving?

I saw myself improving by surrounding myself with positive people who encouraged me to push forward.

What is the key to your healing?

The key to my healing is praying, communicating more, reading and writing.

Will you share what you have learned from your ordeal?

I have learned that keeping things bottled up inside can become unhealthy. Keeping things bottled up has affected my mind and body physically, which in turn has caused me to have different illnesses.

Bitterness

How did you realize you were bitter?

I realized I was bitter when I did not want help nor did I want anyone to talk to me about what happened to my son.

How are you dealing with your bitterness?

I am dealing with my bitterness by being around positive people who are on the same mission as I am.

Isolation

How are you dealing with your bitterness?

I am dealing with my bitterness by being around positive people who are on the same mission as I am.

What does isolation do for you?

Isolating myself messed me up mentally because I felt selfish. I selfishly was not sharing my experience and I soon realized my testimony was to help others get through their pain.

How were you willing to come out of isolation to heal and begin living?

I was willing to come out of isolation by speaking up and speaking out.

Shame

Shame is a self-conscious emotion, typically associated with a negative evaluation of distress, exposure, mistrust, powerlessness and worthlessness. In some cases of shame, some people want to disappear, which can cause inner-directed anger and self-blame. The confusion from being abused often causes victims to look at themselves as the ones to be blamed. From that sense of shame , some attempt to escape chemically by baring a false fault for something that was out of one's control. It wears most people down. Being victimized , the victims victimize themselves by carrying the shame.

" Release yourself from shame."

"Allow not your shame to restrain you"

"From your shame reclaim your dignity."

" Don't let your shame define who you are"

" Shame can drive you insane, forgive yourself and move forward."

" Shame is a burden that you don't have to bear."

Come forward from shame and reclaim your life. You were not born to be down. Refuse to continue bearing the burden of shame. Release yourself and learn to live in happiness. It is time to be free.

Fear

What are you afraid of, that has kept you locked in hurt? I was afraid of myself, I wanted to hurt the person that murdered my son. How are you going to face what you have been fearing? I am no longer afraid to face what I was fearful of I had to realize that the damage was done, God has full control of it all.

Isolation

Keep have you been isolating yourself if so why? I isolated myself because I felt like I didn't need anyone to understand my hurt or tell me the same song. " if you need me I'm here for you"

Growth

Growth is never immediately evident , yet continue to strive to improve and remember change is always at hand though you perceive it not. Dedicate yourself to the goals you have set and remain diligent , you will grow into then person your committed to being.

Know that growth never eludes the truly committed. Either grow or wither away, for nothing stays the same. The question you should ask yourself is " what can I do to help me grow in the ways I need to." You must work on becoming . There are two states , growth and decay . One is conducive to life the other is conducive to death. Life is verified by movement that which is still , stagnate awaits deaths embrace. To grow is to embrace life .

Strive to grow and transform in order to transcend the obstacles that are part of the course. There will always be failures, yet they are nothing except learning experiences that you must grow from.

Acceptance

Acceptance in human psychology is a person's assent to the reality of a situation, recognizing a process or condition (often a negative or uncomfortable situation) without attempting to change it or protest against it. Acceptance is coming to grips with the things you can't change. Assert yourself and do not just let life pass by you, but apply yourself. We must accept the fact that we have power and we are never powerless. There are always parameters within which we must work.

What have you elected to accept?

Accept the fact that you always have options, nothing is set in stone, find your way. If you cannot accept people for who they are, what does that say about you?

What are you refusing to accept?

You are not the only one who wants to be accepted. Everyone craves acceptance. There was a time in my life where I accepted things that were not healthy for me until I realized I was an enabler. At times I thought it was normal to accept excuses for unacceptable behavior. I honestly believe in learned life lessons. I thank God for the storms I encountered, good and bad. Every time we remember something, we relive it. But remember the way we relive it, is never the same twice.

Example: I was going through abuse mentally and physically, mentally by allowing someone to be the master of my mind, physically by allowing someone to beat on me. Did I like and enjoy the abuse? No. Did I accept it? Yes. Did I get tired? Yes. I had to make a change to become happy and healthy. Stop accepting the things that are detrimental to your health. Love yourself, embrace life, and start living.

There is no special pattern for prayer. Simple ask God and go for it.

God, grant me the serenity to accept the things I cannot change, courage to accept the things I can and Wisdom to know the difference.

Focus

Focus on your mental well-being and watch as your physical self improves. Remember it is about you, without you, there is no healing. Resist the pull of foolishness and commit to the pursuit of excellence, stop simply existing and start living- embrace life and make the best of it. Give yourself a reasons to be great. As others can, you can! Nothing is keeping you from becoming what you wish, except yourself. No one can stand in your way unless you honestly believe them, but even then, it is your acceptance that allows it. Stop accepting whatever is hindering you. You are valuable, start appreciating yourself and take care of yourself. No one can define your worth, so go on and shine for yourself, because you are precious. Love yourself and share what you have learned. Smile because the pain can not keep overwhelming you, and it is time to realize that nothing can force you over the edge. Come back you are loved and help is available.

Free

What is free? Free means not under control or in the power of another, able to act or to do as one wishes. How did you realize that something was holding you, arresting your development and depriving you of the life you are supposed to be living?

How did you free yourself?

For me, It has been to help others **"H.E.A.L"**.

"H.E.A.L" stands for............

"Helping. Everyone. Attain. Love" throughout the process from Hurt 2 Healing the truth has been revealed. You are powerful and capable of moving from Hurt 2 Healing. As I am free, I say, "COME OUT YOU MIGHTY PEOPLE !" I am liberated! I am freed of what was for me a disease of fear, of isolation, of bitterness, and most of all, from hurt held in. I was alive yet not living. I could not see it was always on me to liberate, to emancipate myself and in liberation I would truly be able to help someone else **H.E.A.L.**

www.ingramcontent.com/pod-product-compliance
Lightning Source LLC
Chambersburg PA
CBHW081129080526
44587CB00021B/3806